Presented To:

_____

Author's Autograph:

_____

Date / Occasion:

_____

The They Effect

The They Effect

ISBN: 978-0692840740

First Edition

Published in 2017 by Get it Girl Publishing, LLC
Saginaw, MI 48601

All Scripture References are from the New King James Version of the bible unless otherwise noted

Printed in the United States of America

SCRIPTURE

ACTS 3: 1 – 11

"*Now Peter and John went up together to the temple at the hour of prayer the ninth hour.*

*And a certain man lame from his mother's womb was carried, whom **they** laid daily at the gate of the temple which is called Beautiful, to ask alms from those who entered the temple; who, seeing Peter and John about to go into the temple asked for alms.*

And fixing his eyes on him, with John, Peter said, "Look at us." So he gave them his attention, expecting to receive something from them. Then Peter said, "Silver and gold I do not have, but what I do have I give to you: 'In the name of Jesus Christ of Nazareth, rise up and walk.'"

And he took him by the right hand and lifted him up, and immediately his feet and ankle bones received strength. So he, leaping up, stood and walked and entered the temple with them --- walking, leaping, and praising God. And all the people saw him walking and praising God.

*Then **they** knew that it was he who sat begging alms at the Beautiful Gate of the temple; and **they** were filled with wonder and amazement at what had happened to him.*

Now as the lame man who was healed held on to Peter and John, all the people ran together to them in the porch which is called Solomon's, greatly amazed."

CONTENTS

Acknowledgements

Thanks, be unto God for his amazing love and grace that allowed me to write and publish this work. It is beyond my wildest dreams that I would ever become a published author... But God!

To my faithful, steady, patient, consistent, and strong husband of thirty-eight years: We did it! This book could not have happened without your encouragement and your hand on my back! I feel your prayers and I appreciate your love. Always and Forever is more than our wedding song, it's who we are!

To my daughters: You two make me beam with pride every day! I am so grateful to God for allowing me the honor of being your mom. I would tell you two that you can do anything you want in life, but I am certain that each of you already know this and for that I am grateful. Don't neglect to remind my two beautiful grandchildren of this fact every day of their lives. Zai and Alayah you are so special and capable. We expect greatness from you!

To my strong, confident, intelligent, beautiful mother who not only taught me how to be me, but that it is okay to be me! Thanks for your unconditional love and your faith in me. What an example to follow and an ideal model to look up to. I have always looked up to you and that is why I stayed in your closet! Thank you for allowing me to interrupt your baths, sit on the side of the tub and enjoy your company.

To my sisters: Sharon, Vickie, Valerie and Robin. Sharon, you really are my big sister who calls me even when I neglect to call you back and then tell me that you love me! You rock! Vickie I always loved it when you came home to visit: My "Big City" sister with the huge sense of humor, style, and million-dollar smile. Valerie, you are my go to sister. Everyone goes to you with their heart because they know they can trust you with it. You are exceptional. Robin, you pushed me out of the baby sister role, but you are certainly worth it! You are such a wonderful sister and I so love you!

To my brothers: Robert, Lorenzo and Gary. Robert, your intelligence is astounding. Thanks for being my protector and one of the first family members who allowed me to take them to church with me! I love when we gather together, it's always great conversation. Lorenzo, you introduced me to "good" music and the flute! Thank you, I still love good music. I want to thank you both for the *"Last Poets"* and *Gil Scott, "Heron."* Gary, you are my oldest brother who is gone but never forgotten. Oh, how you loved me. I am so grateful to have had a brother who encouraged me, sang loudly with me, and said it was ok to be bold and different. I often think about how uncomfortable it was for you to go through new member's class with me, but you did it, because oh how you loved me! I miss you!

To my dad: You were there during my formative years when my personality was formed. I have always felt you're love, always! You walked me down the aisle on my wedding day. I will always remember that walk. You have always been there in a way and at a time when I needed you. Just this past Fathers' Day, you held your arms out to me in a way I will never forget! I have judged every man by their shoes because of you!

To my mother-in-law: I don't know what it means to have in- law issues, thank you for that. You are every bit my mom! Thanks for your love, encouragement, and support. It is so great to have my mom and mother in law as best friends!

To my Uncle Junior and Aunt Pearl: thank you both for loving me! Thanks for your example of marriage, staying together through it all and loving each other. Looking at you two now encourages me to look forward to the latter years with my husband! Uncle Junior you may not be perfect but you certainly are the Best!

To my sister, Sheryl, we have forty-five years of unbroken friendship. We have evolved through so many stages, but here we are together in the Lord! You are amazing in your capacity to love and serve. From the moment, we met, we were connected for life! We have gone through and made it to the other side.

Bridget, my patient friend of more than forty years. Now that I am finished with this book, I am returning your call! What a great journey we have had and are having! God really did put us together.

Dureen, you are amazing! Your capacity to love and to serve is epic! I am so proud to have you as my sister.

To my entire Transforming Life Church Ministries family: I Love y'all! You guys are the Best!!! Thanks for allowing me to serve you! We have grown and continue to grow so much with each other and the best is yet to come!

To the people who have made an impact on my life spiritually: I am so thankful to God for you: Dr. Lonnie and Lady Frances Brown you helped my husband and I rebuild our foundation. Drs. Ron and Georgette Frierson, what an honor to have you both as our spiritual parents. It is an honor to do ministry with you. To see the growth and favor of God upon your lives and ministry is inspiring. We really don't get out of this relationship alive. We started from the YMCA, now we're here, LOL!!!

Drs. Anthony and Linda Revis, I am so grateful to have attended Arm Bible Training Institute. I knew that I was in the right school when I observed Dr. Revis tear up as he talked about Jesus. What an amazing opportunity to receive the knowledge of the Word along with the anointing! Thank you both! It is because of you that my new and unexpected journey began at ARM!

Margaret "Pearl" Layton, CEO of Black Pearl Publishing, LLC: there is absolutely no way this book would have been completed without your encouragement, inspiration, diligence, and example. Thank you for your prayers that pushed me further than I thought I could go.

FOREWORD

Thought provoking and insightful is how I would describe this book, *"The They Effect,"* by Dr. Laura Brown. Dr. Brown does a masterful job of weaving her journey from what others thought and said about her into who God has shaped her to be and most importantly, who she believes she is.

She shares her personal struggles from being restricted and almost dominated by the opinion of others, even in the simplest of things, to a life of freedom to be all God has called her to be. The result of that journey is the writing of this book to share how wonderful it is to live a life beyond *"The They Effect."* She also shares insights on how you, too, can get beyond what *"they say"* about you.

The book uses personal testimony, narratives, scripture, helpful suggestions and models to enrich the lives of those struggling to get beyond the opinion of others to a position of trusting God's view of who they are. The plain-talk writing style of the book is relaxing and thought provoking, making for a comfortable and inspirational read. The reflections and review feature at the end of each chapter is a plus that helps the reader retain the important points by doing exercises. It is a book that can be simply read or used as a workbook, which contributes to its literary value.

As you work through the book, you feel the personal investment of the author into your life. You also begin to hear the spiritual call that tunes your spiritual ear to the voice of God over the conversations of others. You then start to experience what it's like to wake up to a fresh view of yourself over the biased image that others portray of you. You find yourself emerging from the shadows of opinions of others into the sunlight of the image of God.

I encourage you to read this book, enjoy the stories, embrace the concepts, and be enriched by the scriptures shared. They create a roadmap to deliverance from the potentially crippling effect of what others say about you to newfound spiritual freedom of what God sees in you. Dr. Laura Brown is to be commended for undertaking this assignment to deposit this book, *"The They Effect,"* into the body of believers in Christ.

Dr. Anthony Revis,
Faith Ministries Church, Pastor
ARM Bible Training Institute, President and Chancellor

INTRODUCTION

DISCOVERING THE "THEY EFFECT"

"Who do men (they) say that I, the Son of Man, am?" So they said, "Some say John the Baptist, some Elijah, and others Jeremiah or one of the prophets." He said to them, "But who do you say that I am?" Simon Peter answered and said, "You are the Christ, the Son of the living God." Jesus answered and said to him, "Blessed are you, Simon Bar Jonah, for flesh and blood has not revealed this to you, but My Father who is in heaven..."

The week had been long, chaotic, confusing, and challenging. I remember sinking down in my favorite chair allowing myself to be swallowed up in its familiarity and comfort. I heard myself let out a long sigh of surrender as I felt my body go limp. Simultaneously, I softly whispered, "I can't". I can't say yes one more time, I can't go when I don't want to go. I can't continue to smile while reassuring others, and I can't continue to live my life like this." I did not want to do what "They" wanted me to do another day.

I know I was exhausted but I am sure I heard the still small voice of the Holy Spirit say:
"Who told you that you have to? Who told you that it is unacceptable to be you?"

1

I had not been that startled in a long time, to the point that I had to immediately sit up and take notice. My heart was racing and my breathing was working overtime to calm my heart's pace. I knew at that moment, life as I knew it would change forever.

For me, that day of physical, mental, emotional, financial and spiritual exhaustion began a time of inner inventory, reflection and self-discovery. It would be my first time realizing that I was dealing with influences that had the capacity to affect my character, my emotions, my behavior, my success and my critical life decisions. I characterized these influences as the "They Effect" or what I have termed as "TE."

You see, several years ago, I delivered a message entitled "The Tribe Called They". I spoke to an enthusiastic crowd that seemed to grab onto every word I spoke that day as I talked about how "they" can appear to be your helpers but "they" are actually your hindrances.

Person after person waited to talk to me after the event to thank me for delivering that message and told me how it helped them understand some situations in their lives. I was elated and so thankful to God for the message that day and how it impacted the audience. I saw people walk away lighter, more joyful, hopeful and full of peace.

Little did I know that the same message that I delivered years ago was now here to deliver me. I began to realize how I had allowed the subtle but heavy handed opinions and self- serving expectations of others to zap my energy, joy, confidence, and finances. I had become so focused on helping others, pleasing, praying for, encouraging, and financing the dreams of others, I was utterly depleted and in need of the same help that I had given to so many. I needed personal freedom from "The They Effect."

THE "THEY EFFECT" DEFINED

We've all heard someone say at one time or another:
"You know what 'they' say, don't you?"
"What will 'they' think about your decision? "
The first response of the person being asked these questions may be:
"Who in the world are 'they'? "
"Who are the "infamous they?"
"Why on earth do 'they' even matter? "
In its simplest form *"The They Effect"* can be defined as the opinions of a nonspecific group of people

3

(Known and Unknown) who can be generalized as "everyone," "someone," "anyone," or "them." The "They Effect" (*if you're not discerning*) can influence you to the extent that the impact can keep you from going to your place of wholeness, abundance, and success. Knowing about the "They Effect" is critical in order to discern the influences that are impacting your belief and value system. The failure to discern the dynamics of the "They Effect" influences can trap believers in a cycle of defeat. The "They Effect" captures and blinds our minds with its arguments, speculations, assumptions, theories about our circumstances to influence our deep-seeded beliefs about life, who we are, about whose we are and what is possible for us from God's perspective.

Jesus dealt with the "They Effect" on several occasions. One occasion was in Matthew 16:13-16: When Jesus came into the region of Caesarea Philippi, He asked His disciple, saying, "Who do men (*they*) say that I, the Son of Man, am?" So they said, "Some say John the Baptist, some Elijah, and others Jeremiah or one of the prophets." He said to them, "But who do you say that I am?" Simon Peter answered and said, "You are the Christ, the Son of the living God." Jesus answered and said to him, "Blessed are you, Simon Bar Jonah, for flesh and

4

blood has not revealed this to you, but My Father who is in heaven…"

Jesus was not influenced by what men had to say about who He is because that is the "They Effect" at work. The nonspecific someone, anyone, or them. Jesus wanted to know what His disciples who could hear from God were believing about who He is. Jesus never let the "They Effect" determine His identity. Only the word of God defined and determined His identity, His purpose, and His outcome.

In our own lives, the contemporary "They Effect" that influences and shape our beliefs may involve the environment, credible and non-credible others, repetitious information, and life experiences.

THE KNOWN AND UNKNOWN "THEY EFFECTS"

The "*Known* They Effects" are people you know and afford a level of respect. The Known TE crew is somewhat easy to discern because people you don't know have a limited, if any influence concerning the matters of your day-to-day life. The "*Known* Effects of They" can involve a family member, a friend, and/or foe.

The "Unknown They Effects" is somewhat harder to discern their level of influence in your life because their influence impacts you in an indirect way and may be deceptive or undetected. The "Unknown They Effects" can also involve "specific or nonspecific things" that are accepted by the majority in a group of people or societal norms. For example, The many alternative lifestyle choices.

Sometimes, the Known and Unknown "TE" group can be one in the same. That is because at times, we don't know what we don't know or we are not aware of who or what is affecting us and to what degree is influencing us.

THE DECEPTION OF "THE THEY EFFECT"

Acts 3:1-10, NKJV

Now Peter and John went up together to the temple at the hour of prayer, the ninth hour. And a certain lame from his mother's womb was carried, whom they laid daily at the gate of the temple which is called Beautiful, to ask alms from those who entered the temple; who, seeing Peter and John about to go into the temple, asked for alms. And fixing his eyes on him, with John, Peter said, "Look at us." So he gave them his attention, expecting to receive something from them. Then Peter said, "Silver and Gold I do not have, but what I do have I give you: In the name of Jesus Christ of Nazareth, rise up and walk." And he took him by the right hand and lifted him up, and immediately his feet and ankle bones received strength. So he, leaping up, stood and walked and entered the temple with them- walking, leaping and praising God. And all the people saw him walking and praising God. Then they knew that it was he who sat begging alms at the Beautiful gate of the temple; and they were filled with wonder and amazement at what had happened to him."

In the account of a lame man healed at the Gate Called Beautiful found in Acts 3:1-10, *"They"* brought the beggar to the temple gate daily but never led him "inside" to change his condition or circumstances. The daily routine was a "They Effect" (TE) routine that kept the beggar trapped in a cycle of defeat. He had no expectation that complete healing and transformation could take place. To the undiscerning, it appears that "They" had the beggar's best interests at heart, but a closer look reveals "They" perpetuated and enabled his condition, circumstances and defeatist lifestyle.

"The They Effect" is deceptive. At-a-glance the influences seem helpful, needful, reliable and even vital. However, all influences must be vetted (sanctioned) by every word that proceeds out of the mouth of God (*Matthew 4:4*).

Like the Bible account, we can all think of someone in our lives or we may know someone who uses an individual or group of individuals, knowingly or unknowingly, as a crutch or co-dependency in their lives. For instance, an individual may be trying to kick a drinking habit, but a *"TE"* friend always seem to show up at their house every pay day. A *"TE"* friend will show up to give them a ride to the bank to withdraw money from their account to party and to purchase drinks for the whole crew. However, when the person trying to kick their drinking habit or runs out of money they also lose their *"TE"* friends.

> The "They Effect" is very deceptive.

These same friends from *"The They Effect"* Crew will also take this person to their doctor's visits to get prescription drugs to feed their own addiction, knowing that their friend will "share" his meds with them. At-a-glance and un-vetted, the *"TE"* Crew looks like they are helping the person but they are merely enabling that person's addiction while getting their own addiction fed. *"TE"* relationships seem innocent but are really destructive. They can take many forms such as co-dependency and therefore are very deceptive.

THE PURPOSE

My Purpose for writing, *"The They Effect"* is

- To enlighten or shed a bright light on the characteristics of these influences
- To educate the masses about their tactics, origin, intention, and
- To empower every reader with the knowledge and practical tools to effectively destroy any *"They Effect (TE)"* activity in their lives

I personally discovered the debilitating consequences of *"The They Effect"* in my own life which caused me not to live up to my full potential and to question my ordained abilities and inheritance. In order to substantially help others (with the help of the Lord), I had to break through the wall of unwarranted fear and intimidation. I believe my battle and subsequent success can positively benefit others.

The They Effect Influence

That day while sinking down in my favorite chair, I didn't know that I would begin a journey unlike any I have ever embarked on because of *"The They Effect"* influences. Although I don't think there was anything that I could do to have avoided any of the unknown, unforeseen, and unbelievable events that I encountered along the way to self-discovery; I began to understand, why I could stand and smile in the face of blatant disrespect, disregard, and disdain from the mouth of the self- proclaimed *"TE"* friends.

My greatest discovery or revelation included the unmasking of *"TE"* that I had long since dismissed as unimportant and powerless. In retrospect, I have gained an understanding of how "TE" entered, influenced and operated in my life through life altering incidents that I had dismissed long ago. For this reason, you can imagine my surprise when I rediscovered, how much power and influence *"The They Effect"* had asserted over the course of my life. Unknowingly, I had become a card-carrying member of *"TE"* even though I was loudly and boldly refuting much of their rhetoric.

It began with me making my decisions based on their subtle influence. Even though, I hesitated because my attention was focused on my shortcomings, because *"The They Effect"* focused on them, too. I was accustomed to walking in a tremendous amount of confidence and boldness, until I slowly but surely began to second guess my decisions and intentions. I questioned my purity of heart for helping others because *"TE"* voices were constantly challenging my motives. Finally, I found myself being worn down.

A HISTORICAL PERSPECTIVE

"The They Effect" has always existed; from the moment man received the breath of life, and his flat lungs began to expand with life-giving oxygen, their influence, power, and authority began to flourish.

"The They Effect" was a part of the adoring crowd the moment you were presented to the world. Their voices meticulously blended in with the chorus of other well-wishers, pontificators, and prophets. Each one had a voice of their own which they loudly, proudly, and with

11

unflinching certainty declared your purpose, personality, and probability for success.

"T*he They Effect*" (or *satanic influences*) was present in the beginning, only their voices were masked. "*The They Effect*" was present during the creation, witnessing the marvelous works of God. They saw how God meticulously prepared the earth for man and established man's dominance and remained silent. It was not until God scooped up the dormant dirt, breathed His Spirit, life, and power into man that "*The They Effect*" Crew became restless. It was "*The They Effect*" Crew that spoke to Eve in the Garden of Eden, questioning the directives of God and causing Eve to see and think differently and ultimately turn her back on who she really was.

It was the "They Effect crew" that spoke to Eve in the Garden of Eden.

"*The They Effect*" group establishes itself in your life and thoughts by constantly bombarding you with the familiarity of their voices and opinions. As a consequence, when you have an idea, thought, plan, or goal that causes you excitement to the extent that you know beyond all reason that this is what your destiny, unsolicited voices will emerge simultaneously with opinions, advice, judgments, and views and warnings about a dream they cannot see, hear, or understand.

In my experience, it is amazing how particular voices manage to usurp higher authorities, transcend socioeconomic groups, races, genders, and infiltrate the highest stratospheres of academia. However, because the voices are familiar you listen and automatically consider the plausibility that their assertions may be correct.

Therefore, I am writing this book to expose the most powerful yet invisible and unknown influencers on the earth. It is simply unimaginable that a faceless, nameless entity has the proven ability to change mindsets and life choices with a mere utterance or reference. From the stay at home mom, to the corporate CEO, it is highly likely that the influence of the *"The They Effect"* Crew has already reverberated throughout their home or organization in some manner.

Childrearing, relationships, financial habits, wardrobe choices, religion, and politics all have outcomes that are highly influenced by *"TE."* Consider when a mother decides she will raise her offspring differently than what she experienced and immediately the voices begin to drown out her well thought out rationale. Heavy handed intruders crowd her mind drowning out the memories of the adverse effects of the childrearing tactics she has decided to avoid which wreaked havoc in her own life. Or, what about the husband who decides that he wants to love his wife differently than any example he has witnessed in his life. He makes the decision to love his wife like none other, to go out of the realm of average and deliberately go above and beyond with overt acts of love and service towards her. Once again, with almost frightening immediacy, *"TE"* voices are on the scene with warnings, judgments, and in this instance, ridicule. *"The They Effect"* Crew condescends the notion that this husband presumes to believe he could accomplish what others within his demographic have not managed in previous generations.

Exposing the "They Effect" and providing strategies for the challenges.

Along with exposing *"The They Effect,"* it is my intent to provide strategies and challenges to help facilitate freedom of thought, along with the fortitude to entertain new experiences, exposures, and expectations. A thought precedes every action, consequently it becomes imperative for individuals to possess clarity of the thought process without the intrusion of known and unknown others.

Consider this example: a vast number of people, if not most, base their shopping purchases based on a relationship they have established with a particular brand or product. Yet, "The *They Effect* Crew" (TE Crew) wields unwavering influence without the individual having a specific insight as to their identity. Even though some *"TE"* wisdom has proven unreliable at best, it still maintains loyalty and a vise grip on the minds of many.

As a young woman at the age of nineteen, I was told that the days of getting married at a young age are over, that a marriage of this sort will NEVER last. I was inundated with insinuations and questions about my decision to get married at a young age. It was said that I was either pregnant or a gold digger. While both of these assumptions were untrue, I was not pregnant and there was no gold to dig, the TE Crew continued with their relentless diatribe. This vocal attack was only one of the many encounters I've had with this pesky TE Crew. I somehow had the resilience to ignore the vociferous echoes and opinions as to why it was a disastrous decision to marry so young. Thank God I had the gumption to tune out the interfering and intruding voices of the Unknown TE Crew! I did not have any type of established relationship with these voices, therefore, I ignored them. Because of having

15

freedom of thought, free from the intrusiveness of known and unknown others, my husband and I will soon celebrate thirty-eight (38) years of marriage!

As you learn the intimate details about *"The They Effect* Crew," including their characteristics, motives, intents, and methods, I believe you will walk in liberty, clarity, and power beyond what you can imagine. Let's get started! Let the reveal of begin!

INTRODUCING

THE THEY EFFECT CREW

Let's look closer at the example of the man at the gate called Beautiful. The man is described as being lame meaning he could not have gotten to the gate on his own, he needed "help." Help can come disguised as genuine and pure but beware not to grab every hand that reaches out to pull you up because "they" just might have hidden agendas. While looking closer at this specific account of the friends that brought the man to the gate daily to beg I began to wonder what type of people invest so much of their time on a consistent basis to bring someone to sit and beg? The first thought that comes to mind is what's in it for them, how will "They" benefit? Always take stock of your group, what is the mutual benefit of the relationship?

As I delved into this account further, I came to understand the motives of the friends that carried this man daily to the gate to beg. I realized that there was a monetary incentive for them. The beggar had the right to beg because of his infirmity, therefore, he and his disability were beneficial to his "friends." I don't mean to sound redundant, but it is so important to have discernment or insight into other's motives when they offer to help. Now, most people have good intentions, but, there are those who will try to benefit from your pain, impairment, or hardship, and it is to their gain to help you maximize your present condition rather than to see you made whole.

Much like my earlier example of the person trying to kick a drinking habit, the man at the gate called beautiful was worth more to his friends as a beggar than if he was healed, whole, and knowing Jesus. **Understand, there are people who are sent to gain from your pain, it is their assignment.** The "They Effect Crew" (TEC) are **influencers, intruders, and imaginations.** They

> **Remember, not all angels work for God.**

come dressed in light but their intentions are dark. Remember, not all angels work for God! Therefore, seeing that there are angels who are sent to hinder and not help, you must exercise your discernment to know when to say yes to the help that's offered or to say no.

Just because someone offers you a ride does not mean you should get in the car, there are times when you will get to your intended destination quicker by walking. Relationships can either be stepping stones or stumbling blocks. Family, friends, and foes all play a major role in the "TE." Each one serves a unique and necessary function.

Before I go any further, please note that this book is not about your victimization to the actions and opinions of others; rather it is a guide that will empower you by helping you to realize that within you lies a victor. In the upcoming pages, I will help you to unleash your inner victor as you discover:

1. Who God created you to be, and
2. Gain the fortitude to possess all that He has for you.

BREAKOUT STRATEGIES EXPLAINED

At the end of each chapter you can look forward to a Breakout Strategy. The Breakout Strategy is a call to action, where I will encourage you in an exercise that is geared toward freeing you from the effects of "They" and returning to your authentic purpose.

BREAKOUT STRATEGY 1

EXPOSURE: Exposure uncovers options previously obscured by circumstances.

CHALLENGE: During your first Breakout Strategy, I want to challenge you to try something new! Shop at a new store, try a new gym, meet one new person, take a different route. In other words, go somewhere that you have never been!

TAKE NOTE: While you're on your new journey, take note of your thoughts, feelings and opinions concerning your new experience. While you are enjoying your new experiences, I encourage you to take special note of how you feel about what you think others feel concerning your joy. Taking note of this is intended to get you to identify the members of "The They Effect Crew" who are in your own life.

Answer the questions below:

1. Who are the first people that come to your mind that you feel you must hide your new experiences or happiness from?

2. Next, why do their opinions matter? What do you need from "The They Effect Crew" that should only come from God? (*This could be advice, approval and/or attention.*)

3. Finally, once you've exposed the *"TE"* Crew, take note and embrace your own personal feelings about the experience. Allow yourself to inhale the freedom and exhale all the bondage of the *"TE,"* and what they bring to your experience. Resist the fear of moving out of your comfort zone. Continue to expose yourself to new experiences free of the influences from the TE Crew.

CHAPTER I

THEY EFFECT:
THE FAMILY

THEY EFFECT: THE FAMILY

"The thief comes not but to steal kill and destroy."

(John 10:10)

The "They Effect" (TE) influences individuals by muttering its subtle attacks to parents, siblings, grandparents, aunts, uncles, and other relatives. Breakdown occurs when the entire family unit buys into these attacks. TE's main goal is to destroy the family unit.

"Your adversary the devil walks about like a roaring lion, seeking whom he may devour" (I Peter 5:8).

TE wants to influence, impact, impart, and leave a mark that is not easily erased from your life. Because the family is by far the most important unit of man, the family is on the front line when it comes to attacks by the TE Crew. God intended the strength of the family to be a formidable force against all foes and distractors. While the family is the safety net, it is never the less replete with its set of difficulties and challenges.

Prisons are full of generations of men who are incarcerated because of the affects of They. In the penal system, you will find a man's father imprisoned for selling

24

drugs. Two cell blocks over, you'll find his son is in the same prison for robbing someone to get drugs. In the free world, you will find his grandson is on trial for killing someone for stealing his drugs. We call this vicious cycle a generational curse in the Body of Christ.

This is an example of an entire family that has subconsciously bought into *"The They Effect."* None of the men can probably put their finger on the invisible force that has them bound, but they are none the less influenced by *"The They Effect."*

On a more personal level, I can remember early in my life, conversations with my older siblings when so often someone would tell a story that inevitably included a reference to "they;" what they either said, did, or saw. The conversation would go something like: "Hey guess what they said today," or "You know they say that boys can't just be friends with the cute girls," and my siblings would repeat statements like, "They say you can't go to that school, store, or neighborhood."

I remember having such a curiosity about who are "they?" Although, I never gained clarity on their exact identity, I only knew that "they" were powerful and strong. As the stories went around from sibling to sibling's recollection of a happening, the intensity and volume rose with each retelling. It was an amazing interaction to watch, even though it was confusing at the same time. You see, family and story time is such a cornerstone and a building block, to the extent that whatever elements are involved in the story become impactful. Although, I couldn't fully comprehend who "they" were, I knew these individuals were somehow incredibly powerful, and power is addictive. However, I did not know that "they" were on assignment.

Later, in my walk with God, I had to continually and heavily rely on scripture like:

"If God is for us who could be against us" (Romans 8:31),

To combat this invisible yet powerful force of *"The They Effect,"* God's Word says, *"Wisdom is the principle thing; and in all your getting, get understanding"* (Proverbs 4:7). I realized that my curiosity to know who "They" were also stirred in me a desire to want to know if "They" really knew what "They" were talking about in situations. The elders of old often said, "You can't believe everything that you hear." It was having the wisdom and understanding of God to question the TE Crew's existence and validity that helped me to stretch beyond their limiting and debilitating reach.

26

Imagine a family structure with beliefs built on the wisdom of *"The They Effect."* Beliefs, in general **can be either liberating or limiting.** Liberating if the *They Effect"* has a firm foundation in believing that with God all things are possible. However, beliefs can become limiting when the knowledge of the *"The They Effect,"* is rooted in the negativity of the word, NO:

- No, you can't
- No, you won't or
- No, you had better Not

Coming from a family structure that was considered disadvantaged: a single mother raising seven children, according to "TE," my family was destined for failure.

It was clearly voiced that there was no way we could or would climb out from under the heavy burden of poverty. It was further declared that we would only go so far in our education, and there were substantiated statistics to back their gloomy claims. At one point in our formative years, we lived in the projects, or public housing for low income families, where *"The They Effect"* ruled. As stated before regarding my discussions with my siblings, I can't tell you how many conversations began and ended with, "Well you know what "They say..." I was beginning to feel as if I believed what "They" said. God knew I would need victory over The They Effect Crew. He brought me that victory in creative and unsuspected ways. My first victory over TE came with my love for red lipstick.

MY LOVE FOR RED LIPSTICK

"TE" lingo fell from our lips and the lips of our friends and neighbors easily and freely. For instance, I remember having a fascination with red lipstick (I still do today!), and I was told: "You know what "they" say about women who wear red lipstick?" I didn't know, but I soon found out that day what "fast" meant. That day I learned that fast meant that you were an easy or loose woman who a man could have his way with romantically. I also learned that red lipstick was one of the ways that others identified this type of a woman. Although, that cautionary information didn't put an end to my fascination with red lipstick, I did become careful about sharing my love for it.

I know that it sounds simple that something as minor as liking red lipstick could be influenced by "The They Effect" but this goes to show you how subtle and persuasive the "TE" crew can be. My love for and fascination with red lipstick stems from the admiration I had for two amazingly strong, bold, and courageous women. Like I said, when I was a little girl, wearing red lipstick was considered only for women who were

> **My fascination with Red Lipstick stems from my admiration of two amazing women.**

prostitutes or loose per "TE". Well I was neither loose nor a prostitute and I admired the two women who rocked their red lipstick and lived their adventurous lives like none other! Between the two of these women, I learned early lessons of freedom of choice, love, acceptance, and overcoming!

Never the less, with intentional ill will, "TE" inhibited my curiosity and boldness to embrace my love for red lipstick. You see, within each family, there is invariably a member who will think differently than the majority, much to the chagrin and frustration of the majority members. Inevitably, whenever the bold member offers up an idea, thought or opinion, the "TE" swoops in to shut them down quickly lest their heard. For as long as I can remember, I was described as different within my family. It was true. I thought differently than my siblings. I

29

entertained elaborate dreams and aspirations beyond our meager circumstances.

Now, as the youngest child, if I sound like I am putting my family down for the way that they thought, please know that I realize that my older siblings and other loved ones had experienced and seen a lot more negativity than I could ever imagine. I know that they had a lot more to fight through mentally and spiritually to overcome our limiting reality.

This brings me to my next point, why the saying that, "Knowledge is power" is so true. Hosea 4:6 says, *"My people are destroyed for a lack of knowledge."* I didn't know it then, but it was through God's Wisdom and a desire to know more than our family's mere existence, that I could reach past what I could see. I guess you can say that I was being trained (even as a child) to *"Walk by faith and not by sight" (II Corinthians 5:7).*

Whenever I read a book, magazine or watched a television program, I visualized myself within the context. I lived a glorious life through this media! While reading, or watching a television program, I did not feel the constraints of boundaries or

> **"Walk by FAITH not by Sight."**
>
> 2 Corinthians 5:7

limitations. I only embraced blissful freedom and the jubilation that accompanies endless possibilities! The celebratory euphoria continued until the "TE" reared its ugly head. Suddenly, the frigid waters of whispering voices splashed my thoughts with such a vehement force that it was like a seasoned boxer slapped me on both sides of my face, in an attempt to awaken me from a distant dream.

"They" loudly reminded me of the reality of my immediate surroundings. The solid concrete walls of the "unit" that I called home, the walls that my mother made me and my siblings scrub every other weekend because she didn't want to invite the roaches of our neighbors into our home. In a blink of an eye, I was again face-to-face with reality interfering with my joyful journey.

Was it insane to believe that my temporary address was not my ultimate destiny? According to "TE", the answer is a resounding, "Yes!" Yet, I know that God places us where we can see glimpses of His greatness in the midst of bleakness. Although the voices of "The They Effect" are absurdly loud, God allows us to witness the achievement of a family moving out of the projects going to a "real neighborhood." In the "real neighborhood" one

31

could breathe, dream and be; giving rise to the ever-present hope in you that there is a way of escape!

And, yet I can see the remnants that linger long after the audible voices fade. The "They Effect" is far reaching and long lasting. I recall recoiling inwardly ever so slightly when I was reminded about my surroundings. My eyes were forced to look at my immediate reality. Although, I did not know how to fight back, I certainly felt the urge well up on the inside to resist what The "TE" had deemed my lot in life, with every fiber of my young being. Instead, much like the feelings that I experienced in the chair story that I told in the introduction, I often retreated, feeling:

- Emotionally depleted and wounded.
- Physically exhausted.
- Financially broke.
- Spiritually spent.

I was far too young to experience such a profound sense of loss and defeat. I needed to get back to reckless abandon in the belief that all things are possible. It is in that belief that I found solace, energy, and unrestrained optimism in the midst of constraints, pessimism, and lethargy.

THE RED MUSTANG OF POSSIBILITY

Although, the They Effect Crew's influence is pushy, prominent, and influential there exists those who will push back in defiance, daring to break out and live free. A second bold woman entered my life at the moment "TE" began to wear me down, and I began to entertain doubts. The woman had decided to live differently and not care about the voices, opinions, or detractors. This beautiful, courageous woman refreshed my soul with a ride in her red convertible Mustang!

Like my love for red lipstick experience, this seemingly simple ride in the red convertible mustang did wonders to break me out of the They Effect Crew's influence. I can still feel the wind rip my face as I relished my time with her, in that red

> **The ride in the Red Mustang of possibilities was a welcome respite**

mustang of possibility, a welcome respite from the constant fight with "TE." This bold, beautiful woman also wore my favorite red lipstick with reckless abandon, and I was refreshed and encouraged! She was my personal saving grace from that relentless "They Effect Crew." I relaxed

33

while riding in that mustang, I dreamed fabulous dreams, sang audacious songs, and smiled until my face hurt! It is so wonderful to receive an ice cold drink of hope in a parched desert of mediocrity. It seemed like every time I experienced my jubilant ride, I exited that vehicle stronger, happier, and bolder.

It was as if the woman took on the role of Peter and John in Acts, Chapter 3, and she saw me lying at the gate called Beautiful ready to beg and before I could give voice to the words, she just said look at me. And, "look" is what I did! I looked at how she gripped the wheel of her car, how she tied her scarf securely enough to deny the wind the right to take possession, yet loose enough to allow movement beneath its covering. I began to figure it out! *If I wrapped my thoughts tightly enough in my heart, I still had freedom of movement beneath the overbearing They Effect!*

This began my official tactical intense battle against "The They Effect." I stepped out of the car feeling exuberant and extraordinary, until the time came to walk up to the front door of my home. I opened the door and immediately I heard the tribal voices tell me not to think that I am special, it was just a ride, nothing more. But I

34

knew it was more, much more. It was the beginning of a long-running battle that "TE" and I would engage in for years to come.

It is altogether possible to be fully engaged in a warfare where there is no awareness by other family members. The reason none of the other family members are aware of this tribal battle is mainly because:

- Each member is fighting their own tug of war with "TE."
- One's ability to appear happy most of the time during a struggle.

"Man looks on the outward appearance, but the Lord looks on the heart" (I Samuel 16:7).

Man, is limited in his ability to assess the emotional well-being of another individual. I learned early on that life was more easy going wearing a smile. Needless to say, I smiled often. Actually, for the most part, I lived in a state of happiness. Despite my meager upbringing, I enjoyed life.

It was "TE" that reminded me often that life wasn't so great. TE always had a hard slap of bleakness despite the hope of an amazingly bright and energizing future. I had to be schooled about what it meant to have to live in the projects, and all the implications and stigma that my address implied. At the time, I loved our bright orange door at 1904 Syracuse! We didn't have our father in our home, money was tight, and family members were upset, depressed, oppressed and repressed. However, **in the midst of this negativity, sometimes the deficits become accepted and are normalized.** The loud arguments become framed as our culture, or our unique way of communicating and the lack of encouragement became our way of toughing one up for the realities of a hard life ahead.

A FANCY FEAST FOR FOURTH GRADERS

Albeit, in the midst of hard circumstances, God always managed to position someone in my life to shift my focus to Him and He wants to do the same for you. There might be a whole "They Effect" Crew against you but God needs to send only one person to shift you. I was fortunate enough to have a fourth grade teacher who recognized my academic potential, and she took it upon herself to nurture me, I was able to achieve at my individual pace through a system of self- study and she recommended that I skip ahead a full grade. This excellent and selfless teacher also introduced our entire class to fine dining and etiquette.

She exposed me to the world I had no idea existed. You see the strength of "TE" lies in keeping the truth hidden, but God will always make a way of escape for you (see I Corinthians 10:13). This dear, bold teacher took it upon herself to remove the limits, expand the expectations, and experiences of a group of African American "Project Kids." Imagine the sight of a group of fifteen or more African American fourth graders walking into one of the best restaurants in our city in 1968!

My Mother allowed me to wear one of my church outfits for this occasion. I only wore my church clothes for special functions. So, I just knew that this trip was

> **My 4th grade teacher exposed me to the world I had no idea existed.**

considered, "A big deal!" It was considered out of the ordinary because we were taking a bus trip across the bridge that acted as a racial divide in our city. Also, everyone was super excited because my fourth grade class was going to sit and eat in a restaurant that the majority of our parents had never stepped a foot on its property. Most of our parents didn't dare dream that they could actually sit at a fine restaurant table complete with formal linens and place settings, not to mention actually eating a meal there.

As the yellow school bus pulled into the parking lot, my excitement was almost impossible to contain. My eyes grew wide with anticipation and I could not control my wonder of it all! The table setting both amazed and confused me. I was excited and intimidated. I had not seen such a grand setting. The array of utensils made me dizzy and I had no clue on how to correctly use them.

You see in our household, we made use of jelly jars, unmatched dishes, and an assortment of mitch-matched forks, spoons, and knives. So, this type of exposure was eye opening yet bittersweet. While my eyes were opened to new ways of doing things and possibilities, I knew that:

- The restaurant experience would come to an end.
- I would have to return home and face my reality.
- I would no longer feel the same contentment.

Our restaurant experience that day helped me to learn about something different, and I loved the difference. Oliver Wendell Holmes Sr. said, *"One's mind, once stretched by a new idea, never regains its original dimensions."*

38

From that day forward I dreamed a bigger dream for myself. Hey, I was able to:

- See life lived without caution in bold beautiful red lipstick.
- Experience a freedom ride in a Mustang convertible.
- Eat lunch at a fancy restaurant.

> **From that day on I dreamed a bigger dream for myself.**

Surely, my life was meant for grand things! The only thing that cast doubt on this super dream life I envisioned for myself was my return home. After each new encounter, I returned home to the voices of "The They Effect" Crew. Although my mind had been stretched by a new idea, "TE" dogged me with realities, innuendos, and intimidation. It was a constant fight, until God intervened once again. Because of the effort and diligence of my Mother, our financial situation greatly improved when she graduated from nursing school! After my Mother graduated, we moved to a brand new neighborhood away from the projects!

Yes, my family was now the family that achieved! We moved away from the projects to live in what I called a "real neighborhood." My newly stretched mind was ecstatic to encounter new family examples and experiences that matched my dreams, and with the freedom to give voice to all of my hopes for the future. Although the echoes of "TE" were present, the voice of hope and resilience spoke louder and was more dominant.

In this chapter, like me you should have discovered that exposure is a useful tool in the fight against "The They Effect". "The They Effect" Crew attempts to limit, while exposure reveals opportunities and options. Because I now recognized options, I felt a surge of both power and freedom, and you can realize the same exhilaration. Here a few strategies and challenges to encourage you as you defeat "TE."

While In most cases, the family is the go to sanctuary for the individual members. My goal for writing this section is to reveal how a unit as sturdy and hearty as the family, is still not exempt from "The They Effect" Crew and how through exposure that family unit can overcome "TE's" influence.

BREAKOUT STRATEGY 2

PART 1: <u>Explore diverse families</u>. Notice the many ways of interaction, see what seems familiar and what is different. These families can be found at church, at restaurants or in a shopping mall. Take note of the interactions that appeal to you and incorporate them into your family structure. **NOTE**: DO NOT TRY TO FORCE QUICK CHANGE in your family: You will encounter resistance; try one change at a time.

CHALLENGE: Invite a family that you admire out to dinner or to your home and ask them what they love most about their family and take note of the answers and interactions.

PART 2: Over appreciate your family! Most folks want to feel special; it tends to bring out the best! Call, text, or send a card of "just because" appreciation. Every genre has a superstar in its lot; why not be the Starbucks of appreciation within your family?! You set the bar for all the others to reach.

CHALLENGE: Send a special card to a family member today with a handwritten note of appreciation on the inside.

CHAPTER II

THEY EFFECT:
THE
NEIGHBORHOOD

THE CORNERSTONE OF HUMANITY

"...You Shall love your neighbor as yourself..." (Matthew 22:39)

Just as the family is man's foundation, the neighborhood is the cornerstone of humanity. The neighborhood is comprised of an extended set of parents, grandparents, brothers, sisters, aunts, uncles, and cousins, as well as friends. This neighborhood is the place where attitudes and opinions are formed that potentially last a lifetime. The neighborhood is the intended place to supplement the nurturing that under ordinary circumstances take place within the family and the home. Sadly, many neighborhoods are no longer the safe havens they once were.

Gone are the surrogates that watched over all the children as if they were their own. I remember well the chorus of voices that reminded me it was time to get home before the street lights came on. I can also remember getting gentle reminders from my elderly neighbors to make sure I told my grandma my whereabouts and to play nicely.

When I was a child, children were esteemed highly, and they were taught to show that same regard for the elders. There was plenty of food to feed more than the immediate family members. The neighborhood was the playground, safe place, social hub, and life's training ground.

THE NEIGHBORHOOD IDENTITY

Each neighborhood where I resided had its individual character. The areas with the family unit intact were more upbeat, hopeful, affirming, positive, protective, and prosperous. The freedom to roam and explore was exhilarating. My first neighborhood was very territorial. I was given careful instruction not to stray into areas where I was not granted specific access due to territorial and attitude barriers.

Crossing boundaries in my old neighborhood came with dire consequences. Threats were made and fights were the norm. Even though, my new neighborhood was indeed entirely different in demographics, it was the same as the old neighborhood, because the voice and influence of

"TE" resounded in the new neighborhood just as loud and powerful.

I found it quite puzzling to move to a place that I thought was a safe haven from "TE" only to discover that they took up residence in more than one area. It took some time, but I came to an understanding of the origin of "The They Effect." Their voices emanated both internally and externally. Internally they spoke through the recollection of previous conversations and rebukes. Although discussions come to an end, the effects are long lasting and life changing. Therefore, when new opportunities are presented, the tendency to hesitate steps in. Living life cautiously begins early on, but not cautious in play. On the contrary, our life of play knew very few boundaries, but rather in believing greatly. I have learned that the neighborhood will either serve to elevate or suppress.

I recall being invited to become a member of a girl's singing group, even though, I did not feel that I was much of a singer. The other members of the group were fantastic musicians and they wanted to coach me along because they felt that I had solid potential. Our coach was the father of two of the members. Their dad was extremely encouraging even though I doubted my singing ability, I looked forward to the weekly sessions because it was full of positive affirmations.

I am smiling as I write this portion of this book because I can vividly recall the emotions associated with that experience. The most efficient deterrent to the adverse effects of "The They Effect" is positive reinforcement and experiences. If you can put together enough positive experiences, you can withstand the negative onslaught of "TE." You see experience crushes doubts. Engaging in mind altering experiences brings you closer to your destiny as you break out of your arena of comfort.

Although not maliciously, the same environment that so lovingly nurtures can also smother. Dreams are in danger of being smothered by fear. "The They Crew" calls this protection. You see, the way that "They" influences the Neighborhood is it appears that "They" don't want you to suffer hurt or disappointment. Their "protective instincts" cause them to strongly advise you to tone-down your dreams and to put them into proper perspective, so to speak. This is where experiences become vitally important. Positive experiences serve as a buffer against the onslaught of safe advice.

Once you have allowed yourself the opportunity to launch out into unfamiliar territory, whether you succeed or not, you are never quite as content with being comfortable. It's akin to wearing your favorite pair of jeans after you've outgrown that particular size, you might get them back on but they are hardly as comfortable as they once were. You see, it's like joining the singing group that invited me to be

Being comfortable is not always profitable.

a part of their dream; because of that experience I learned to be confident in my abilities and unashamedly acknowledge my shortcomings. After being a part of that singing group, I no longer felt comfortable in my comfort zone. Being comfortable is not always profitable. At times, it is detrimental to your progress and/or success.

The neighborhood also taught me about expanding the definition of family. The elderly couple who becomes grandma and grandpa even though they don't share the same DNA. I have adopted sisters, brothers, aunts, uncles, and cousins galore from the various neighborhoods that have left their indelible mark on my life. From the middle school student teacher who with a sharp rebuke, reminded me not to allow my mouth to run (ruin) my life, but at the same time encouraged me and assured me that I possessed a beautiful mind strong enough to control it (my mouth); to the counselor that found it difficult to believe that I was raised in a single parent home because of my personal presentation, social and academic abilities. I have to admit, initially I took offense to the counselor's comment. I felt that it demeaned the substantive effort my mother took in raising my siblings and I. I later (*much later*) lovingly embraced the assessment as an open look at the inner work that I manifested in my life. I never wanted to make my mother look bad (something I was taught in one of the neighborhoods), so I consciously worked hard to make a good impression.

THE MENTORING MANTLE

During my time in the neighborhood, I learned another tactic employed by "TE": to take you to it, but to never take you through it or in it. Imagine someone dangling a cure for your sore leg in front of your face. They tell you all of the awesome benefits, give you amazing testimonials, yet, they will not allow you to use the product! The product exists, it works, and it is available, just not for you. This omission is one of the ways "TE" operates. They will tell you or show you the evidence of the good life but not give you the information about how to attain that life. They will assure you that freedom from your bondage is possible, but will not show you the way to attain it.

Some inhabitants of the neighborhood know how to succeed right where they are but refuse to share the formula. They will invite you into their home that happens to be the best one in the neighborhood but will decline to teach you how to replicate their success. Implication without implementation leads to desolation. In other words, success is implied but there is no substantial instruction on how to actualize it in your life. This can cause a sense of bleakness, frustration, and despair.

I recall a conversation I had with a very talented craftsman. I complimented him on his fine craftsmanship and he began to tell me that there were very few people who knew how to do what he did really well. I instantly felt a sense of loss and I asked him, would he be willing to take on an apprentice?

His immediate response was, "No!" Alarmed at his quick negative response, I asked him, "Why not?" He explained how expensive his machines were and how he didn't believe that a young person would be able to grasp the intricate processes of what he does. I probed deeper and I asked if he felt a responsibility to:

- Share his craft.
- Leave a legacy.
- Keep his craft alive.

His response was somewhere along the lines that he was self-taught and that another person would have to learn for themselves also.

Now, I have to admit I felt anger and indignation begin to well up on the inside of me, so, I ended the conversation. Before I left him, I sternly reminded him that he learned his trade from someone before he taught himself the intricacies of his craft, either by observation or invitation.

You see, there was a time when the neighborhood took the mantle of mentoring seriously. The "Neighborhood" folks took great pride in teaching what they knew. If someone in the neighborhood noticed a young man struggling with academics they began to teach him a skill that would feed him. On the other hand, there were mothers, grandmothers, aunts who made sure a young man going off to college had basic skills that would help pay his tuition, such as ironing, washing, or cooking.

Sadly, the voices in the neighborhood have weakened to a more pessimistic tone.

THE HIDDEN TRUTH

IN PLAIN SIGHT

Many would not have survived and flourished if the vocal tone of the neighborhood was as negative then as it is now. The difference is measurable when you compare the attitude of the generation that benefitted from the familial nurturing protecting neighborhood versus the generation that grew up in the self-centered, jaded hands-off community. Unfortunately, there is one particular crew that is sinister it its tactics and relentless attacks. This certain group will work tirelessly to obstruct successes in the neighborhood. Their voices rise above the rational discourses as they spin their convincing tales of discontentment, despair, and discouragement.

The belief of life being hard and unmanageable is solidly reinforced as they recount over and over their disappointments and failures. The stories are spun in such a way it seems that failure or coming up short is inevitable.

52

The tone and tenor mingled with unfeigned emotion makes it difficult to withstand the onslaught of loss. The "TE" speaks through those who:

- Look like you.
- Had your same ambitions, goals, and dreams.
- Hit the wall of failure with a fierceness that annihilated every ounce of courage you managed to muster up.

That's what "TE" does, beat its opponent down with consistent negative dialogue.

Magnification of one's failure serves to blur the other successes causing it to become second nature to give attention to the one who did not reach the mark. The truth is often hidden in plain sight. We find our eyes diverted away from the glare of success, while, our attention is fixated on the ones who did not make it. It's akin to complaining about the one eyesore house on the block while ignoring the beauty of several other homes with pristine well-manicured lawns. You know it's like a phrase that is repeated over and over until it becomes a mantra such as folks going around loudly proclaiming "the struggle is real!" Well, of course a real struggle exists, but so does a very real victory!

BURDEN AND YOKE BEARING

You might be carrying the wrong burden and yoke!
I asked someone recently, "What factors attributed to the
confidence that you display in your life?" What I wanted
to know is if the neighborhood had any significant impact
one way or another. This person had great basketball skills.
I asked, "Has there been a particular person or persons that
encouraged the development of your skills?" It was
astonishing to see this person struggle to pinpoint when and
where the encouragement began. To help get his ideas
flowing, I flipped the question and asked, "Would you
mind sharing with me a negative situation?" Ironically
enough, the memories seemed to flow quickly and freely of
how he and his friends encouraged one another in negative
situations.

While the situations that he mentioned were not
what I wanted to focus on, the details he recalled were
precise and vivid. After I pointed out that acts of
encouragement were present within the group to do wrong
deeds; suddenly, memories began to flood his mind about
some positive influences that took place in the
neighborhood. For instance, a man asked this same group

to join his basketball team. The man saw their potential and wanted to encourage them to embrace their abilities and reach for the best. He was also able to recollect how he and his friends encouraged one another to get into the water and learn to swim. Understand, during his childhood, not many neighborhoods had ready access to a swimming pool. Therefore, many African American children did not know how to swim. So, going to a swimming pool was both a treat and a challenge. Imagine hearing your friends calling out your name inviting (no, challenging you) to jump!

I took the opportunity to point out the fact that their neighborhood was actually a source of encouragement that helped to lay a foundation of confidence in their life. There are times when the "noise" of disappointment and distraction silences our memories of encouragement and can result in undue burdens or yoke bearing. This unnecessary weights are mostly brought on by becoming comfort in one's current condition.

How Does Comfort Coexist
With Negativity?

"Can anything good come out of Nazareth"
(John 1:46)?

One can easily fall into the trap of comfort. These comfort traps look like negativity carried within the community. How does comfort coexist with negativity, you may ask? Comfort exists because there is the absence of a challenge to jump. Comfort lacks movement beyond the self-imposed and/or inherited boundaries.

In this comfort zone existence, one may be tempted to think something like, "I may not be where I would like to be, but at least I am comfortable with the familiarity of my situation." I've seen, experienced and embraced it all before. The voices tell you things like:

- "This is your allotted portion of the good life."
- "Be grateful."
- "It could be worse."

As stated before, couldn't things be so much better? Better is not only available, if you will jump, it is visible and attainable. To achieve better, you just have to move your

56

eyes away from comfort and negativity and focus on the dreams you have that require taking calculated risks. **Taking calculated risks and living the very best you can wherever you are, is both a skill and a gift.**

Consider, when Jesus began his earthly ministry. The question was asked "*Can anything good come out of Nazareth*" (John 1:46)? Perhaps you've heard the same inquiry concerning your neighborhood. The answer has to be a resounding. "Yes!"

Truth be told, I am from the neighborhood or "Hood," as they say in the African American Community, where struggle, difficulty and mediocrity are the norm. Who would have expected such power, grace, wisdom, authority, and love could come from such an underwhelming place? What the neighborhood skeptics failed to realize is that Jesus did not come from Nazareth, He came from glory! Nazareth was merely a temporary station in life, a starting place for human reference.

THE PROMISE: BETWEEN THE PROCESS & THE OUTCOME

"The They Effect" mindset will try to convince you that where you begin is where you will eventually end up. The truth is that you and I may not have had a say about where we started, but we have a huge say so as to where we will end-up. The promise is achieved after going through the process. You need to know that **it is in the midst of going through the process that "The They Effect" is most vocal and forceful.**

Oftentimes, there is a void between the promise and the process. This is known as a "space in time" where we can't see what will happen from our current positions to our future outcome. The sad thing is that if no one shares the intimate details of the in between steps, we are frustrated in our process. Frustration sets in because we begin to think that our journey to the promise is uniquely different from everyone else. The truth is, "there is nothing new under the sun" (Ecclesiastes 1:9). Our situation is "common to man" (1 Corinthians 10:13). None of us are exempt. We will all go through the human experience known as life.

To be clear, struggle is not unique by any means. Quite the contrary, struggle is very common. The struggle began when:

- We tried to make it safely through the birth canal as our mothers bore down with each push in pain, hope and anticipation.
- We took our first steps as toddler.
- Matriculated through the school age, teenage and adult stages.

No matter where you were in life, the struggle has been constant and consistent. **It does no good to compare one struggle to another, just know that it is universal and is a necessary component of the process.**

There is a scripture that encourages us to:

"Count it all joy when we fall into various test and trials" (James 1:2).

These tests and trials are also known as the process. Why? Because, **it is in the midst of the process that we learn the value of the promise and we mature enough to obtain that promise.**

As I look back on my many struggles that I have faced, I am beginning to appreciate the process more than ever. I have come to understand how *"All things work together for my good"* (Romans 8:28).

I know that the politically correct thing to say is, "I wouldn't change a thing, even if I could." Truth be told, there are a few things I would undoubtedly correct. Yet, I still see how they worked together in my process to help me arrive at where I am today. Though, at times, the struggle has been real, I am so grateful to have gone through the process. It is the process that has allowed me to arrive in the place of victory that I live in today.

MEDITATING ON THE MEMORIES

"I understand that we are not to remember the things of old neither consider the things of the past because God is doing a new thing in our lives that shall spring forth now" (Isaiah 43:18-21). However, when it comes to filling the void between the process and our promise, meditating on memories are essential.

When "The They Effect" tries to have you come up short in obtaining the promise because the process is too difficult, you have to remember you have gone through tough times before. I have memories that I refuse to allow to slip away. Today, when I am faced with financially trying times, I briefly meditate on memories of the time that I had to leave groceries in the store because I did not have enough money. I remember that just as I made it through those times God will get me through any current financial hardships. I know that our God is the "same yesterday, today and forever" (Hebrews 13:8).

By meditating on these memories, I am encouraged to continue this life's race to the finish! I can't begin to count how many times the memory of my entire family living with my aunt and uncle, at least fifteen people in a four bedroom house, surfaces in my mind. We slept two to three people per bed. I was graced to sleep with my mother and my sister. That living experience made it so easy for me to open up my home to homeless and/or needy family and friends when the need presented itself.

Before opening my home to those in need, the voices of "TE" spoke loudly and said, "No, don't do it!" My experience and perspective reassured me that even if the living arrangement ended badly all things would work together for my good.

NURTURE HELPS TO ENHANCE NATURE

You see, my memory of the neighborhood functioning as surrogates is ingrained indelibly in my heart and I am eternally grateful and indebted to the many co-collaborators in my life. Co-parenting is a contemporary term that has its roots in many neighborhoods that have benefitted my life in unmeasurable ways.

Nature or Nurture is a long running debate among academia but for me it is simple. **Nurture helped to enhance my nature.** Nurture

> **Nurture helped to enhance my nature.**

overcame the negative presuppositions and predictions of failure based on my beginning. I have also benefitted from having some of the most giving, loving, non-judgmental, courageous, and strong women that I have ever met actively nurturing me in my life.

EXAMPLES AND EXPERIENCES

These guidance, wisdom and examples I have received from these women are with me with every tough decision I encounter. When the voice of impending failure attempts to rise at decibels that can shatter glass or drowning out the loudest sounds of locomotives, it is important to have examples and experiences to reinforce what you know to be true. **You can make it to the other side of the process.**

In my neighborhood, I have witnessed countless women:

- Make meals appear from nothing.
- Return to school mid-life.
- Look disappointment square in the face, while shaking their fists, determined to make it.

Their resolve shocked the nay-sayers by their successes.

I don't know when the neighborhood took such a turn to a negative tone. I don't know when the perception of impending doom took hold of the hearts and minds of so many of the neighborhood's residents. Perhaps it was the circumstances that piled on such as the:

- Realities of life.

63

- Devastation of death.
- Differences of opinions in a divorce.
- Uncertainty that comes with a job loss.
- Adjustment caused by relocation.
- Feelings of abandonment by children going away to college and not returning.

As you can see, there are multiple reasons for the downward spiral of the once beloved and highly esteemed neighborhood.

In the old neighborhood, parents and other family members pooled their money so that a child or children had the chance to experience opportunities beyond the immediate neighborhood. Because my "Neighborhood" folks raised my enrollment costs, I was able to participate in:

- Dance recitals,
- Bands,
- Camps, and
- Choirs.

> **The experiences I was privileged to engage in helped to shape my life**

Much of the expenses were shouldered by more than one family member. Young people looked to the neighborhood to help finance special field trips through the purchase of candy, candles, and cookies that they did not need. In many cases, they not only didn't need the items sold, they did not want them. Unfortunately, today many neighborhoods turn a deaf ear to the plea for help from the young person seeking diverse experiences that will expand their capacity to dream a bigger dream.

The experiences I was privileged to engage in helped to shape my life in such a manner that I had no choice but to have a vivid imagination.

SHARED EXPERIENCES

Experiences will raise the level of expectation. Experiences open the eyes to a previously unknown level of possibilities. Another great aspect of the neighborhood is shared experiences. Family and neighbors easily share negative experiences. But it is the sharing of positive experiences that will off-set these failed and intimidating realities.

Imagine if one person who experiences great success shares with the other families in the community the blueprint for his or her ascent. An enlightening example is a young person that becomes the first in their family and or neighborhood to graduate high school. Not only do they graduate but they perform well academically and socially.

The desire to continue their education creates both excitement and fear for the young person and their family. The lack of money becomes a secondary concern once the young person rakes in scholarships and grants. The family is now confronted with a new fear of whether the young person is equipped to deal with the complexities and choices that come with being a part of a new neighborhood, a community with different choices, expectations, and opportunities.

> **Imagine if one person who experiences great success shares with the other families in the community...**

On the other hand, an equally gifted young person who is socially adept among his or her peers is also facing fears of the unknown college experience. Even though, this person had many diverse experiences, he may not have ventured from his immediate peer group. Unbeknownst to either party, the root of their fear was identical. Neither had previous experiences of being outside of their environment; or the experience of engaging with a group of people who are not like them. The young person who is socially adept among his peers that share the same experiences, social norms, and expectations, is equally unprepared as the young man with limited experiences

Consequently, fear of the unknown will cause some self-sabotage. The inner voice of courage is overtaken by boisterous "They Effect" rhetoric. Therefore, it is important to amass enough outside experiences no matter how uncomfortable. These new experiences act as a buffer against the unrelenting thought tirades trying to convince you that your dream is impossible to accomplish. Having a past experience to hang your hat on gives you the empowerment needed to achieve beyond your comfort zone. For example, the experience I had with the singing group: It is because of my involvement in that uncomfortable endeavor that I gained a substantial amount of confidence that serves me well today. You must know how to embrace your abilities and accept your shortcomings. You don't need an overwhelming amount of experiences, just enough diverse ones. Experiences are great teachers, if, we learn the lesson and apply the knowledge.

Imagine the same young man going off to college armed with having the experiences of interacting with a broad spectrum of people. How different the outcome is sure to be because his confidence level is certain to be higher than the young man with limited experience with unique groups. Embrace the experiences presented to you

67

they can literally change your life's trajectory for the better!

BREAKOUT STRATEGY 3

Experience is an event or occurrence that leaves an impression on you. Take on a new perspective about the experiences you have journeyed. I want to encourage you to look at them with a fresh attitude and realization that "All things work together for your good" (Romans 8:28).

CHALLENGE: Think of a past experience that has influenced your life's trajectory. Now take a moment and plan a new experience that will further you on your path or purpose by doing the following:

1. Plan a trip to a new place, location. Don't worry about the money, just go ahead research and plan the trip and trust God to provide (see Genesis 22:14).
2. Sign up for a class that is outside of your comfort zone. Maybe it's singing lessons or a swim class. You may even want to write a book! Whatever it is, try it now!
3. Think of one positive experience that makes you smile. Now, recreate that experience as close as possible.
4. Buy a book that will help you attain and experience your goal.

Trying something new can be intimidating. Push past fear and try the new experience anyway. In doing so, expect to:

broaden your horizons and attract and motivate others to do the same!

CHAPTER III

THEY EFFECT:
THE MINDSET

RENEWING THE MIND

Romans 12:1-2 (NKJV)

"I beseech you therefore, brethren, by the mercies of God, that you present your bodies a living sacrifice, holy, acceptable to God, which is your reasonable service. And be not conformed to this world, but be transformed by the renewing of your mind, that you may prove that is that good and acceptable and perfect will of God."

As we have discussed the influence of "The They Effect" as it relates to family and the neighborhood, we begin to understand that "The They Effect" is a mindset that must be transformed, managed and skillfully handled. Therefore, we can renew our minds by:

- Redirecting our perceptions.
- Understanding our journey.
- Acquiring new information.

We redirect our perceptions from that which appeared to be totally devastating by opening our minds to the reality of "the learning opportunity" within the adverse experience. Each experience carries with it two opportunities: one to discourage you on your journey, and the other to propel you to your destiny.

Discouragements arises from a lack of understanding that not all bad happenings come to derail you from your destination. Quite the contrary, some trying, difficult, hard to deal with situations come to strengthen you on your journey, pushing you to continue.

For example, I have learned along the way how to be happy and content living in a household with two large families in small quarters and to have fond memories of that time. I learned valuable life skills and lessons that serve me well today. I have empathy for those who are currently in a similar struggle while being able to rejoice with those who have worked themselves up and out of such hardships. I have learned that contentment and happiness springs from within and is not extrinsically tied to a person, place, thing or happening.

Can you imagine the euphoria the man at the Beautiful Gate (see Acts 3:2) experienced, once, he "looked" --- "focused" on the right people, who had his answer and did not indulge in his infirmities (and try to financially profit because of them)? I am not saying the man did not have actual infirmities but we can do harm while attempting to do some good.

Bringing the man to the place of healing and not leading him in to get healed year after year, causes him to beg for that which will not sustain him, rather than, look for that which will heal him and sustain him. It's the difference between health and healing. Thank God, healing is available for those who need it but it is much better to be in good health and not need healing. **In other words, people may come into your life to help or hinder you. Often times, the two look identical!**

HINDRANCE OR HELP?

Understand that a hindrance is anything or anyone that impedes your successful completion of a task, goal or the intended outcome. The "TE" Crew often thinks, albeit incorrectly, that they are doing someone a favor by not getting their hopes up too high. You'll hear of some people talking about other's pipe dreams that will never happen. "They" will make comments meant to deter the dreamer, not because the people are mean-spirited, quite the contrary, the deterrent is to protect and shield.

So, "The They Effect" begins defensive maneuvers such as not engaging in conversation that encourages, but rather purposefully downplays or degrades the dreamer for daring to believe. You must understand that rather "TE" is being initiated by the family or the neighborhood, neither is the problem nor solution but it is the mindset and influence of these inhabitants and influencers. Remember that *"...the weapons of our warfare are not carnal but mighty in God for pulling down strongholds..."* (2 Corinthians 10:4-5) **Who are the major players in your thought life? Whoever you grant permission to influence your life will take full advantage of the invitation.** Some people foolishly mistake the median income of the family and neighborhood for their average intelligence, influence, and impact. There is not a family or neighborhood that is exempt from the "The They Effect's" influence and impact. The influence seeps subtly but deeply and swiftly. If not careful, before you realize it you utter a hidden thought you didn't realize was inside of you.

THERE IS POWER IN REPETITION

How did this latent thought get into your psyche and become part of your beliefs? By virtue of being an inhabitant of a group, neighborhood, or family positions you to accept that group in thought. The more you hear something the more likely you are to become what you

75

hear. The strength of "The They Effect" is repetition. Getting others to repeat a thing whether true or not, gives "The They Effect" it's power. It becomes truth for the hearer because if enough people say it, people now assume the truth has been established. Of course, this is not the case, wars have begun because of a repeated lie and the hearers' willingness to believe it. Recently, a presidential election was won because of repeated lies and the hearer's willingness to believe lies instead of facts.

I often wonder what causes one to buy into something that they know cannot possibly be true. I mean you have clear examples before you that demonstrates the fallacy of the lie and yet, some will still run with the lie rather than go with the truth. I always felt that once exposed, the lie has little to no power. Later, I found this is not necessarily true. If, just one person embraces a said lie, it now has the ability to negatively impact their lives. I believe this occurs frequently within our families and neighborhoods. A lie is told, repeated and believed. Choices are then made based upon that lie.

As I mentioned before, the lie that one cannot achieve beyond a certain level is purported often in certain demographics. Even though there are countless examples to disprove and expose this debilitating lie, it still persists and manifests disastrous results. I am not sure once a lie spreads, or once it is exposed, whether the truth can still emerge in the family and/or neighborhood. It is as if the people are kept in the dark. Or, perhaps it is easier to cling to the lie and not have to live up to the truth. **No matter how daunting the task may appear, the truth will always yield the best results.**

I could go on and on about "The They Effect" and how it affects the family and neighborhood, but remember this: both the family and neighborhood has the ability to elevate you to greatness and help you realize your dreams or suffocate you into mediocrity and dash desires in the name of love. Be mindful!

Each neighborhood that I have lived in and/or visited, I have experienced different emotions. While my parents were still married and living together, I lived in my first neighborhood. Family togetherness is what stands out in my memories associated with that time. I recall family dinners, all my siblings and parents at the dinner table. Sometimes we liked the food choices, other times not so much, but we had to eat what was provided. My dad was a stickler for that idea. He was a stickler in other areas, too. I also remember that my dad's closet had all of his clothes neatly hung and most importantly his shoe collection was all lined up and perfectly shined.

For me this neighborhood was all about families, my own and the many others. The lasting impression that I got from my first neighborhood "TE," kept me dreaming.

THERE IS SAFETY IN NUMBERS

The one thing I don't recall about this particular neighborhood was having an awareness about the negative influence of "The They Effect." I didn't hear their influence or feel their presence. I ponder on this fact and I realize, the more secure you are the harder it becomes for "The They Effect" to exert its influence. So it's the safety of numbers and trusted others that shield you from the evil influences that come to sway your mindset and confidence. I understand all too well the impact of feeling unsafe and vulnerable to mental attacks in other neighborhoods. Attacks that come to knock you flat on your back, suck the oxygen from your lungs, but not allow you to cry.

It is a steady bombardment of can't, won't, and impossible. Understand this, these mental battles must be fought. It will seem as if some will be lost but the war must go on. During these times, you may be tempted to feel totally alone, not one person left standing in your circle. Now What? "For He Himself has said, 'I will never leave you nor forsake you'" (Hebrews 13:5).

This is important to know when you turn to ask a question and there is no one there; or when you scream and no one hears. You will need to muster up the strength and reassure yourself that you are never alone. You will need to be strong enough in the very midst of devastation to remind yourself that you or someone else has been here before. Remember, *"No temptation has overtaken you except such as is common to man, but God is faithful, who will not allow you to be tempted beyond what you are able, but with the temptation will also make the way of escape..."* (I Corinthians 10:13). You thought you were alone and trapped, but suddenly God will show up.

I remember that feeling so well while walking to a local grocery store with a friend, I was around 11 or 12. We were approaching the entrance to the store laughing having a great time. Suddenly, from nowhere a young man walks up to us and grabs me by my arm and roughly pulls me away to the back of the

> **I was thinking why is this person pulling at me and my shirt?**

building. I screamed or I thought I did. My skinny arm began to flail. I was desperately trying to get back to that carefree moment of laughter and abandoned joy. I saw the horror on my friend's face as she ran into the store to get help while the guy continued to pull me towards the back of the store. I had no idea why he would do this. I was young, and oh, so skinny. Why me?

My heart felt like it was going to burst out of my chest. The pounding sounded so loud, why couldn't he hear it? He kept saying, "I'm not going to hurt you!" But, I was hurt and he was hurting me! I kept thinking, "Why am I here alone and why is this person pulling at me and my shirt?" I have no idea how much time passed. However, just when I thought I had no one to help me, help arrived on the scene and pulled me to safety.

My friend's dad pushed the person away from me and pulled me to safety (*I remember thinking I wish it was my dad who saved me*). I was an emotional wreck, I kept thinking, "Why? What did I do or say to provoke such an attack? Did I say something wrong to this guy or wear something wrong, what?" I don't know why but I realized that even in my most dark, scary, devastating and life threatening moment, I was not left alone to be utterly destroyed.

80

The attack was meant to reduce who I was: carefree, full of laughter and joyful. Immediately, the voices began to tell me I had to make an adjustment to who I was. The message I heard was: Don't be so comfortable with who you are, become shy and withdrawn, be ashamed of your body, it got you into this trouble. Up to this point, I was boisterous, jovial, confident and oh so loud!

I was helped into the store and calmed down. The strangest thing is, I almost immediately calmed down. There was no long drawn out histrionics. I simply got myself together, had a cold pop and a bag of chips and got some candy to go. I hopped into my friend's dad's car, went home and never repeated the story. I was done with it, so I thought.

But how does one experience trauma and not have some of the vestiges of the incident? I walked away from the incident physically unharmed, but I was affected. I just didn't recognize it at the time. When, I walked away from that situation, I made a conscious decision to withhold myself emotionally. I did not allow my emotions to be the seat of my control. I heard a voice speak to me to closely guard myself. No one needs to be that close.

Although we experience devastating circumstances in our lives, it is important that we don't live a life of devastation. Sure, I was violated and traumatized and I experienced the aftershock of that circumstance. However, I did not allow that one occurrence to dictate the direction of my life. Through much prayer and by the grace of God, I was able to reestablish a mindset of healthy trust towards strangers.

> **Recognize the tricks and the temptations of the "They Effect."**

As discussed, be mindful that "TE" speaks loud and forceful in the two most important, impactful, and influential voices in our lives: our families and our neighborhoods. Be vigilant about what you hear, know where the information is coming from along with the intention behind it. Recognize the tricks and temptations of "The They Effect." Finally, seek God to overcome traumatic instances in your life that affect your mindset.

⭐ BREAKOUT STRATEGY 4

Take the time to assess and reconsider your inner circle, who are "The They Effect" members that attempt to influence your mindset the most?

CHALLENGE: Thinking about "The They Effect" members who attempt to influence your mindset the most, answer these questions:

1. What does "TE" have me thinking? Am I thinking on things that are pure and good or does evil and bad things cloud my thoughts?
2. What does "TE" have me saying? Am I speaking faith filled words or negativity? Am I saying what I can have or what I don't have?
3. What does "TE" have me seeing? Am I seeing victory or defeat? Do I see opportunities or limitations? Do I see the goodness of God?
4. What am I doing? Am I engaged in activities to increase my life? Am I going to mind-expanding places? Am I serving others? Am I serving God?
5. Do I feel supported? Do I feel challenged to improve and increase?

CHALLENGE: Buy a giant coloring book and paint outside the lines in bright colors and laugh out loud!!

CHAPTER IV

AFFECT THEY: PROPHESY!

"TALK TO IT!"

So Jesus answered and said to them, "Have faith in God. For Assuredly, I say to you, whoever says to this mountain, 'Be removed and be cast into the sea,' and does not doubt in his heart, but believes that those things he says will be done, he will have whatever he says."
Mark 11:22-23

There are times in our lives when things seem to be stagnant and at a complete halt. The joy of living life seems to have waned and the excitement about what's next is non-existent because of uncertainty. When we are at a stubborn place of complacency, fear, depression, doubt and unbelief, we tend to shut down. We don't want to talk or want to be talked to, we just want blessed quietness! Yet, shrouded within the silence is a raging storm of noise that is relentless. This noise is in pursuit to bring you down to utter destruction. Your most powerful defense against the barrage that is coming against you is that you open your mouth and talk to it! Speak the Word of God and prophesy your way out of the dry valley into the land of life.

The Prophet Ezekiel looked upon a desolate place filled with dry bones, segmented bones, broken bones, and useless bones in a vision. God asked Ezekiel a profound question: *"Son of man, can these bones live?"* Ezekiel looked at the fragmented bones pondering the question that he knew the correct answer could only come from God (see Ezekiel 37:1-14).

Has anyone ever asked you a question that you had no clue of the answer or more importantly why they inquired of you? There are times someone with greater knowledge than you will ask a question of you that requires you to recognize that their wisdom is greater than yours.

PROVEN WISDOM

Ezekiel was wise enough to know only God knew the answer and he was humble enough to inquire. What do you do when life is so confusing and overwhelming that you know you have no ready answers? You turn to someone who has **proven wisdom.** Wisdom that has saved others from going over the edge and shown the light in many dark, secretive lives.

Upon staring at the situation and looking at God, Ezekiel spoke **out loud** what he was feeling inside: *"Lord, only you know"* (see Ezekiel 37:3).

At times, it seems like our lives are so complicated and confusing that only God himself has the answers to correct the onslaught that infringes on our joy, peace and existence. The wisest thing we can do is to throw up our hands in surrender to the Lord. God's profound answer is: *"Prophesy to these bones" (see Ezekiel 37:4).*

You see, most often we look at our problems and we don't talk to them. During the instances that we do speak to our problems, we speak the wrong words.

Keep in mind that words are powerful and they are "The They Effect Crew's" only weapons. Words are extremely effective. There was a time when it seemed that an unrelenting barrage of attacks were fast and furiously coming my way. I never verbally hit back, instead, I found myself going silent. The world says silence is golden, but I can tell you that silence can be deadly. Understand that it is not words alone that have power but it is the

> **God's words give you new life.**

spoken word that is most powerful. Unleashed words will change your life. God's Word spoken out of your spirit has in it the ability to create new opportunities and turn around the direst of circumstances. God's words give you new life.

God answered Ezekiel with an amazing response, "Speak to the bones." In other words, what God was telling Ezekiel was "Command those dead bones to live!" It is empowering when someone in authority grants you the right to free yourself and cause your hopes, dreams, and dead situations to come to life again. At the word of God, Ezekiel began speaking and the bones began to line up! Bone upon bone and in perfect order each bone connected and became functional again.

This says so much as it pertains to speaking the right words. When we speak the right words to our circumstances, we drown out all the negative jargon and poisonous conversation from "The They Effect" crew. **Life giving truth trumps defeatist lies every time!** I have experienced such joy seeing my circumstances turn around.

I can identify with the joy Ezekiel must have experienced during this miraculous encounter. There was a season in my adult life when it felt as if I was unaccepted and unwanted. I had a time of walking alone and it was extremely uncomfortable. During this time, I determined I was going to learn to be content with the present while believing God for my expected end. During this time, my finances were challenged along with my health. I began to speak the word of God loudly to myself and declare I was already out of my situation. God sent the right people at the right time to come to my aid. Just when it appeared that there is nothing but the dry parched desert all around you, just one command from God changes everything.

The key is to speak to your bleak circumstances against all of the conventional wisdom of "TE." They may tell you that:

- All hope is lost.
- You are not being realistic by speaking to what seems to be a dead situation in their eyes.

I encourage you not to allow yourself to go deathly silent concerning the obstacles in your life. Doing so will cause your hopes, dreams and visions to shrivel up and die.

WHO OR WHAT
ARE YOU SPEAKING TO?

You may ask, now that you know that you must speak, "Who or what am I speaking to?" Below I will give you the three people , places or things, you are to speak to:

```
           ┌─────────────┐
           │   Talk to   │
           │  Yourself   │
           └─────────────┘
             ↗          ↖
┌─────────────┐      ┌─────────────┐
│ Speak to the│ ←──→ │ Speak to the│
│  Mountain   │      │    Enemy    │
└─────────────┘      └─────────────┘
```

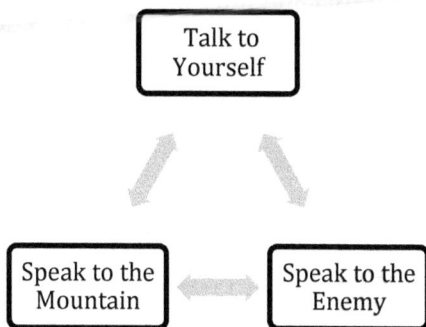

1. **Talk to Yourself!** Talking to yourself will be one of
the most liberating exercises you will participate in.
Before you think that I am being spooky, I want to
encourage you not to think that talking to yourself is
strange. We talk to ourselves all the time. Many times
we do so without realizing it. For instance, when I shop
for shoes, I can tell you that a serious conversation
takes place! I talk to the shoes that I plan to purchase,
so much so, that when I leave out of the store with my
shoes, we have already established a relationship! I tell
you those shoes already know what place they hold in
my life: their importance, function, next outing and how
they will be coordinated with my wardrobe.

Begin to talk to yourself. Instead of repeating the
negative language of "The They Effect," begin to tell
yourself:

a. I shall live and not die and declare the works of the Lord (see Psalm 118:17).

b. Everything that God has planned for my life is coming to pass.

c. None of my dreams will die before they manifest!

d. I am an overcomer! I might walk through a dark time or valley but I will do so fearlessly knowing that I am not walking alone!

e. My situation is temporary and is not unto death. Anything that that I see with my natural eye is subject to change (see 2 Corinthians 4:18). (*If you need confirmation of this truth, just look back over some of your old pictures for confirmation! For example, I like to use my many different hairstyles. I might go the hairdresser with a short pixie cut in the morning and leave that* afternoon with long flowing beach waves! Remember:

    i. "All things are possible to those who believe" (Matthew 19:26)

    ii. Joy is life's best medicine, and

    iii. A big belly laugh in large doses will hasten the recitation process!

2. ***Speak to the Mountain:*** Whatever your mountain of
   adversity is don't just look at it, SPEAK to it! Tell it in
   FAITH that it must be removed! Turn and walk away
   and rest in the promises of God! That mountain has no
   place in your life. It only serves to **hinder, harass,** and
   to **hound** you relentlessly in an effort to get you to give
   up and surrender. When you begin to speak God's
   Word, no matter what your mountain is:

   a. Finances must show up!
   b. Sickness and disease bows down to divine
      health!
   c. Fear must give way to faith!
   d. Overdue manifestations must come forth in
      Jesus' Name!

Your only job is to keep on speaking to the mountain, until
it is removed!

3. ***Speak to the Enemy:*** Remember that "TE" is not your
   friend. Keep in mind that they come to "steal, kill and
   to destroy" (See John 10:10). The goal is to steal your
   joy, kill your dreams and visions and destroy your
   confidence. So you must **remind your enemy that
   you do not walk in fear but in faith and that you**

have a sound, intact, able to reason and discern mind (1 Timothy 1:7). The Holy Trinity (Father, Son, and Holy Spirit) is much greater than the They Effect. Do we need to explain more in depth the Holy Trinity? The Father, who created the world that is conducive to your success, who created you and called you good, and has given you dominion. The Son, who came as a living example of God and how to live a life of dominance through dependence and obedience to God's Word and total surrender even unto death. The Holy Spirit, who reminds us daily who we are in Christ, what we have and what we can do, while showing us the great things God has in store for us!

Now is a good time to rehearse all your previous victories no matter how small. These small victories come in the form of things you do in everyday life like:

- Completing a task on time.
- Resisting the urge to overeat or overspend.
- Making a phone call you were previously hesitant to make.

It doesn't matter the type or size of your victory, speak it over again and again!

Now that you know who and what you are speaking to, I want to share with you three action steps that you must take daily to silence the "They Effect." These steps involve:

1. *Knowing*- You must have a working **knowledge** of the Word of God.

2. *Saying*- You must effectively **say** the right Word for the situation.

3. *Believing*- You must firmly **believe** the Word of God that you speak will come to pass.

DO I REALLY KNOW?

Oftentimes, I hear many people give their opinion about someone or something because they feel they *know* the person or situation. The truth of the matter is (*in most cases*) they don't actually *know* the person or situation at all. A more accurate statement would be that they have read or heard about the person or situation.

For example, many people talk about their favorite singers, or actors, etc. as if they are good friends with them. Think about the outpouring of grief and the firsthand accounts that are told from their followers. The sad part about it is that nine times out of ten, the events never even happened.

On the other hand, when you "really know:" you will have firsthand accounts because of time spent, you will have intimate knowledge of the person or situation. The same holds true for the Word of God. Knowing **about** the Word is not equivalent to knowing the Word. Knowing "about" the Word of God has the connotation of being surface knowledge and requires no depth. While, actually knowing the Word of God will take study and time to have in depth knowledge.

When you study God's Word you make an effort to acquire knowledge. This knowledge is acquired by:

- Daily reading God's Word.
- Daily researching God's Word
- Daily asking the Holy Spirit to teach, reveal, and instruct you.

Study makes you strong, confident and bold. When you are comfortable with what you know, who you share the knowledge with is never a problem. Study helps alleviate embarrassment. Most people do not want to be ashamed because they don't know enough to effectively share. As a result, they become silent. As you can see, it is imperative to **know the Word of God before you say it.**

YOU WILL HAVE WHAT YOU SAY

I know this action might sound redundant, but, the more you say the Word of God the more you will have what you say. The Word is your daily nourishment and fuel for your victory. If you can **transform your words, you can Change your life. Words have power, but it is the spoken word that brings the manifestation of your desire to your life. You must speak life to live victoriously, abundantly, and joyfully. The Word of God is life and therefore, you must speak the Word of God to live.**

BELIEVING FAITH

If you can believe, all things are possible (see Mark 9:23). To believe is to have confidence in the truth, the existence or the reliability of something (the Word) without having absolute proof (Your physical evidence).

"Now faith is the substance of things hoped for, the evidence of things not seen (Hebrew 11:1).

We believe many things in life and we act out of what we believe. Have you heard the saying "actions speak louder than words?" **Actions are derived from what one believes. If I watch how you act, I'll know what you believe.**

Faith is acting on what you believe. Believing faith is described in Romans 10:8-9:

"If we confess with your mouth the Lord Jesus and believe in your heart that God has raised Him from the dead, you will be saved. For with the heart one believe unto righteousness, and with the mouth confession is made unto salvation."

RENEWING THE MIND

When it comes to prophesying (speaking) to "The They Effect," knowing, saying, and doing will require that you renew your mind. God's Word reminds us to be renewed in our minds. Romans 12:2 reads:

And do not be conformed to this world, but be transformed by the renewing of your mind, that you may prove what is that good and acceptable and perfect will of God."

Renewing your mind requires that you meditate on God's Word. We have already discussed studying God's Word. While study is a form of meditation, meditation is also synonymous to muttering, reflecting and seeing God's Word manifested in your life.

"This Book of the law shall not depart from your mouth, but you shall meditate in it day and night, that you may observe to do according to all that is written in it. For then you will make your way prosperous, and then you will have good success." (Joshua1:8).
Once you have knowledge of God's Word, begin to say and believe God's Word. I want to encourage you to visualize God's Word manifested in your life.

This offers motivation to continue in God's promises in the Word, when you can't physically see them manifested. It also offers a quiet confidence when the negative voices of the "TE" try to convince you to give up hope.

Now get ready to put what you've learned into action in your next Breakout Strategy!

BREAKOUT STRATEGY 5

Search the scriptures and come up with your favorite "I can" or "I am" confessions/affirmations.

I'll get you started:

1. I am a child of God (Galatians 3:26).
2. I can do all things through Christ who strengthens me (Philippians 4:13).

Now that you get the idea, use your Bible's concordance or your favorite devotional and write seven more of your favorite scriptures below. Be sure to make time to read and recite them daily until they become a part of you! Go ahead, Get started!

3. _____

4. _____

5. _____

6. _____

7. _____

8. _____

9. _____

CHAPTER V

AFFECT THEY: CHANGE YOUR MENTALITY

CHANGE YOUR DIRECTION NOT YOUR DREAMS

*"For I know the thoughts (plans) that I think toward you,
says the Lord, thoughts of peace and not of evil,
to give you a future and a hope."
(Jeremiah 29:11)*

In Part 3, we have talked about how *"They" Effects The Mindset.* During this section, it is my goal to instruct you on how to flip the script and *Effect They* by *Changing Your Mentality!*

There was a young girl who knew she was different from most people around her. She thought differently, dreamed different dreams, saw unusual visons, and spoke with authority and clarity. The young girl enjoyed her life, until it happened. Somehow, someway "TE" invaded her mentality and suddenly her life changed. What do you do when life gets in the way? You change your direction, not your dreams and vision.

Focus on the end results, chart your course and follow it but don't quit. Remember, because the "They Effect" mentality is one of defeat and retreat, gloom and doom, and fear, its inhabitants will try and encourage you to stay in the box even if you have outgrown the box and it is stunting your growth. If you are not careful, you will be tempted

not to live up to your potential and pursue your authentic
self. This is the enemies trick to try to get you to take on
the mentality of the "They Effect."

AUTHENTICITY

You hear a lot these days about authenticity, but.
really what is it? My definition of authenticity includes
daring to live great in the face of mediocrity. It means
telling the truth in a world that doesn't accept truth, and be
willing to walk your path alone.

A conversation happened at a beauty shop where
the women were talking about a certain female celebrity.
These women stated how arrogant and cocky they thought
the celebrity was. They thought that she was full of herself
and hard. This conversation touched me to my core. After
listening for a while, I simply asked the question, "If she
were a man would you come to the same conclusions?"
After a bit of soul searching, the ladies unanimously said,
"No. "I reminded the ladies at the shop that we have got to
stop this undressing of our sisters. It's almost as if we are
leaving her lingerie to air out in public. You see the goal of
the "TE" is to get us all to attack anyone who does not

think or act exactly like us. We must refuse to use the weapons of the enemy to tear down a sister. Slander, criticism, gossip and accusations are weapons of "The They Effect." Refuse to pick on your sisters and join the fight for our sisters against the accusations of "The They Effect" crew.

I very often hear comments about myself, describing me as a strong woman. For the most part, it is not meant to be a compliment. But, no matter what others say, I have discovered that it is the will of God that I:

- Walk in all my strength!
- I keep in mind that I am made in His image and likeness!
- I know that I am fearfully and wonderfully made and designed for excellence!

In other words, I must be cognizant (that no matter what others think or say) I am good!

CHANGE A MINDSET NOT PEOPLE

The more we behave like God the less we are understood. I am not saying I am perfect. As a matter of fact, I am far from it! What I have realized is that the more

I walk in my authentic self, the closer I am to His image and likeness, and this is the most effective tactic to defeat "TE." The same "TE" that was present during my birth is the same "TE" that met me at the front door after my liberating ride in the red mustang. The same "TE" that tries so hard to keep us silent is "The They Effect" we can defeat by knowing who we are, accepting who we are, and giving the world our true selves.

Not everyone will accept us and that's okay. We are in good company. Jesus was not accepted and so many others that have chosen to follow Him and His example are not accepted. Therefore, we are in the Lord's company and that is a good.

Remember, we don't fight flesh and blood. Note that "The They Effect" is not flesh and blood, it is a mindset that influences flesh and blood. When we lose sight of 2 Corinthians 10:4:

"For the weapons of our warfare are not carnal but mighty in God for pulling down strongholds, casting down arguments and every high thing that exalts itself against the knowledge of God, bringing every thought into captivity to the obedience of Christ..."

We begin to lose the battle and become drawn away from the real fight. Ephesians 6:12:

"For we do not wrestle against flesh and blood, but against principalities, against powers, against the rulers of the darkness of this age, against spiritual host of wickedness in the heavenly places."

It is so important that you know the true foe and defeat him with skillful use of our weapons. Ephesians 6:13:

Therefore, take up the whole armor of God, that you may be able to withstand in the evil day, and having done all, stand.

Never fall into the trap of fighting on the enemy's turf and using his weapons. Know your weapons which are not carnal because we are not fighting people, indeed, we are fighting a mindset. A mindset is defined as the established set of attitudes held by someone. The "They Effect" is a mindset that limits and inhibits and that tries to cloud your authenticity and greatness.

One of my all-time favorite songs is Barbara Streisand's rendering of "Don't Rain on My Parade!" I love everything about the song. The force of will in Barbara. The determination to live life to the fullest regardless of who disapproves, and the willingness to take whatever bumps that might come. She is reminding folks it's her life to live and not anyone else's! Read the lyrics, I can almost guarantee you an instant lift! As a matter of fact, look up the original video on YouTube and see if that doesn't encourage you to tune out the "TE!"

Let's be clear, YOU are the most effective deterrent to "The They Effect" takeover. Your determination and willingness to be your authentic self without regard to the labels other well-meaning and not so well-meaning folks have tagged on you is the ticket to fully living. **No one lives a full life that is being defined by others.**

God has an original design for your life and you will never live satisfied if you allow fear to stop you from fulfilling His original intent. Your life takes on greater meaning when you live intentionally by taking every thought captive, investigate it and either hold on to it or toss it aside.

It is unprofitable and dangerous to allow unproductive, negative thoughts to flood your mind, crowding out the thoughts that are good, productive and useful. All words have an intent. Words will either do good or do harm. Therefore, you will need to be vigilant about the words you allow to linger in your mind and take root in your heart. The words that you keep will either make you stronger or weaker, it's your choice. The words that you keep will develop your mindset. Therefore, for any foul, slanderous, and unproductive words "TE" speaks over you, it is your job to affect "TE" by filtering them through the Word of God holding onto only those that are good, productive and push you towards your destiny. In this way, you effect they through changing your mindset and becoming your authentic self.

BREAKOUT STRATEGY 6

CHALLENGE: Mind your Mouth Manners. Words are powerful and they create. Be mindful of what you say and what you don't say: Death and life are in the power of the tongue and you will live to eat whatever negative (or positive) words you say!

1. Keep a journal of your conversations for 14 days.
2. Notice the times you are speaking positive and negative words.
3. For every negative word, add a pound. At the end of the 14 days add them up: how much weight did you gain?? The word tells us to lay aside every weight... (See Hebrews 12:1).

LOSE THE WEIGHT: Replace every idle word with productive ones: rewrite your conversations.

CHAPTER VI

FREE TO BE ME

A LETTER OF APOLOGY

So, now the decision is made and the instructions are clear, it's time to live free! Alive to your authentic self and dead (doorknob dead!) to the opinions of others. You don't have to shake off the attacks of others because they don't stick to you. If you have the Word of God, you have an impenetrable Teflon shield around you and the deadly attacks slide off, not causing any harm or damage. I had to think about this.

Now, that I am living free what's next? I felt the urge to apologize to myself for all the wasted time, energy, and emotions given over to "The They Effect." I need to make amends with myself and live loudly, proudly, and boldly. I want to share with you a letter that I wrote to myself:

Hey Laura,

I was thinking about you today, as I often do, and it occurred to me that I owe you a heartfelt apology. I am so sorry that I allowed fear, intimidation, along with the vociferous opinions of others to drown out your voice and force you into the shadows. I am immensely sorrowful for the times when you dared to be bold, fearless, and sensational and I talked you into playing it safe while settling for mediocrity. I regret that I did not reaffirm you enough, encourage you more, speak louder to you and for you, and shelter you better from the unmitigated attacks from "The They Effect."

I should have spoken up sooner when their voices attempted to distract, detour, and discourage you along your journey. I could have stood firmer in the belief that you were and are strong enough to endure any vile, vicious, or violent onslaughts against your purpose. I should have reminded you during all the times that you sucked it up, took one or two on the chin, and kept moving in love towards your expected end, that not only are you tough enough but you are also loved enough, you are cared for.

I don't know if you knew that I have always in all circumstances rooted for you, I wanted you to win, to succeed, and to soar. Girl let me tell you, I love your drive, ambition, and your willingness to go THERE, even in the face of fierce opposition.

I love how you take risks in life, love, and work. Obstacles become your stepping stones. You have learned to carefully navigate although you have endured some cuts and bruises along the way. I love how you pour on the oil of gladness and continue the journey even if you have to walk alone, you have learned to master the solitude and revel in the silence. I love how you are embracing the process while going through the maturing season, intent on learning the important lessons along the way. You never cease to amaze me how you see victory in the eye of defeat. You really are my girl!

So, Laura this is what I want you to do: every time you look in the mirror, I want you to see my smile of approval. I approve of your strength and fortitude. I approve of your commitment and steadfastness, I approve of your choice to BE YOU! So, as you choose your hair for today, whether it's to be short or long, blonde, black or brown, curly, wavy, or straight, I approve. When you rare your head back and let loose with one of those life affirming belly laughs, know that I approve and I am laughing just as loudly with you. And Laura, as you glide on that confidence inducing, saucy red lipstick that makes you smile and lights up your entire face, I want you to remember that life changing ride in the red convertible mustang, top down and the wind whipping through your hair, caressing your face just enough to remind you but not strong enough to break you, and know: I approve of you and I deeply apologize. Now, go, DO LIFE!! I Love You, Laura,

All my Love!

With this letter I declare "The They Effect" a defeated foe. And, whenever "they" attempt to rise from the dead, I have a beautiful reminder that no matter what "THEY" say, I am loved and approved! And so are YOU!

YOUR TURN:

Write a letter to yourself. If you need to apologize to yourself, do so and then affirm who you really are. Don't be shy. Say all that you need to say and then put it away in a safe place. Refer to your letter whenever you need to be reminded about your amazing, awesome, audacious self!

CHAPTER VII

THE GOD EFFECT: KEY TO VICTORY

THE GOD EFFECT

Although it is clear that "The They Effect" is powerful, persuasive, and persistent, there is another power that is above all powers. This power is mightier and without limitation. This power is known as God Almighty and the Holy Trinity and is omnipresent, omniscience, omnipotent and the Bible says:

- Creates something spectacular out of nothing at all.
- Brings order to chaos.
- Snatches light out of darkness.
- Makes the ground stable beneath your feet.
- Sets boundaries for the waters.
- Causes the dry places to yield your necessary food.
- Gives you a compass in the sky to control your days and nights.
- Reminds you that night must give way to a new morning.
- Provides life in the air, land and sea and made everything into a perfect environment for success.

The Holy Trinity dusted the dirt from the ground and created you and I! I find it absolutely amazing that we were not allowed on the scene until the earth was made conducive to our achieving greatly. We were not introduced to a dark, confusing place with no plan, purpose, or preparation. From the beginning, God knew that our success was inevitable and imminent. Even though, after the fall of Adam and Eve in the Garden of Eden, we were not exempt from disappointment, discouragement, or at times despair, but, we were nevertheless perfectly formed to win.

The Holy Trinity or triune God includes:

1. The Father.
2. The Son.
3. The Holy Spirit.

The Trinity collaborated to create a systematic plan of development for us whereby we would thrive and not simply survive. Just as the Trinity has a **system of success,** the Trinity did not leave you without that system as a roadmap. If you will follow the instructions given, success is guaranteed.

How then do you walk in the realization of success in your life? The answer is quite simple. All you have to do is, "BE." As you live out your human experience, it's easy to strive to accomplish multiple goals, only to become frustrated in your pursuit. The good news for you is that you don't have to struggle. You only need to, "BE." Be your original design. Fulfill your original purpose. Know that you have the full power of the Trinity working on your behalf. The Father, Son and Holy Spirit not only worked together in creation, they developed a plan that is fail proof when the instructions are followed. There is even a backup plan just in case you fall short. That plan is the plan of Salvation, Romans 10:9-10:

"That if you confess with your mouth, the Lord Jesus Christ and believe in your heart that God has raised Him from the dead, you will be saved. For with the heart one believes unto righteousness and with the mouth confession is made unto salvation."

DARE TO BE

The word "BE" can be used:
- To indicate the identity of a person or thing.
- To describe the qualities of a person or thing
- To indicate the condition of a person or thing.

The word "BE" helps you to know your identity and that you:

- Are created by God and adopted into His family. You are a son/daughter of God.

120

- You are an heir with all the rights and responsibilities.
- You have a great inheritance.

"Being" means that you are legally adopted by God with all the rights and privileges as a natural born son. Not only that, but God has a responsibility to make proper accommodations for his heirs according to His own riches. God's responsibility to you includes:

- Loving you.
- Caring/providing for you.
- Teaching you.
- Protecting you.

Once you know God's responsibilities, you begin to understand your authentic qualities and that you are:

- Made in the image and likeness of the God.
- Fearfully and wonderfully made. Meaning that you were inspected for excellence and have God's stamp of approval.
- Tremendously created and fashioned by God.
- An original creation with God's awesome handprint on your life.

These qualities help you to realize your true condition as God intended for you to be outside of the imposter, "They

121

Effect." The Trinity (The Father, Son, and Holy Spirit) helps you to realize that:

- You are whole.
- You have a sound mind.
- You are victorious.
- You can do all things.
- You are an overcomer and finisher.
- You are a winner.

Today, do not struggle to become, just BE boldly empowered!

BOLDLY EMPOWERED

"So, here's what I want you to do next. With God helping you, take your everyday, ordinary life -- your sleeping, eating, going to work-and walking-around-life-and place it before God as an offering. Embracing what God does for you is the best thing you can do for Him. Don't become so well-adjusted to your culture that you fit into it without even thinking. Instead, fix your attention on God. You'll be changed from the inside out. Readily recognize what he wants from you, and quickly respond to it. Unlike the culture around you, always dragging you down to its level of immaturity, God brings the best out of you and develops well-formed maturity in you. (Romans 12: 1-2, MSG).

When you embrace the Holy Trinity, you realize that The Holy Trinity has soundly defeated the "The They Effect."

MANIFEST

The only thing left for you to do is to manifest all that you have seen, heard and learned that fulfills your destiny. It is not enough to discover the problem. Now, you must implement the plan of action to overcome. You know the truth, and it is a known truth that it is what you implement that makes you free, John 8:32:

And you shall know the truth, and the truth shall make you free."

Act on the truth you believe. Think free, speak freedom, live free. The world was created for you, now produce!

BREAKOUT STRATEGY 8

Search the Word for any and all scriptures that confirm your victory.

Say the scriptures out loud as you write them and insert your name as you read aloud. Confess the Word of God.

Build a victory wall and attach the scriptures on the wall on note cards or sticky notes.

FINAL THOUGHTS

Today, I congratulate you for your bravery in discovering "The They Effect" and having the boldness to break out of the limits that "TE" has placed on you. The journey in writing "The They Effect," has allowed me to become totally free, confident, and bold in walking in the plan of God for my life. I am living triumphantly while wearing my red lipstick and blue hair without apology! I challenge you to embark on subtle boldness in your everyday life that will help you to break away from "The They Effect" and embrace your calling according to the Holy Trinity (the Father, Son and Holy Ghost)!

IT'S YOUR TURN!

www.ingramcontent.com/pod-product-compliance
Lightning Source LLC
LaVergne TN
LVHW021347080426
835508LV00020B/2158